✳ how to mix 200 cocktails

essentials

*how to mix 200 cocktails

essentials

carlos of raffles

foulsham
LONDON • NEW YORK • TORONTO • SYDNEY

foulsham

The Publishing House, Bennetts Close, Cippenham,
Slough, Berkshire, SL1 5AP, England

ISBN 0-572-02821-0

Cover photograph by James Jackson

Printed in Great Britain by Cox & Wyman Ltd, Reading, Berkshire

Contents

Introduction

Cocktails are lively and sociable, with the focus firmly on fun. Once enjoyed by only a favoured few, they are now served in bars and clubs everywhere. There are literally hundreds of recipes for cocktails and each one has almost as many variations. However, there is no great mystery to mixing cocktails, and making – and inventing – your own couldn't be simpler.

This great collection contains many of the classics and a few of the popular modern cocktails that you may have enjoyed in bars and clubs. The recipes are all made up of well-known ingredients – they don't include obscure spirits or liqueurs that are only available from a specialist supplier and which would probably lurk at the back of the cocktail cabinet until they were passed on to your grandchildren as curiosities!

Each recipe makes enough for one drink, unless specified, but it's easy to increase the quantities if you are serving a crowd.

So dip in, experiment and, above all, enjoy!

Your Cocktail Cabinet

Many of the ingredients you'll need for making cocktails are spirits, wines and mixers that you probably already have in your drinks cabinet. You may need to stock up on a few extras, but don't rush out with a long shopping list and spend masses of money just to have an impressive supply in your cupboard. It's much more fun to start by trying out a few cocktails that use your favourite ingredients, then gradually add to your collection if you really get bitten by the cocktail bug.

Alcoholic drinks

The drinks in this first list are used as the basis for many of the recipes. Of course, you don't need to buy them all at once; start with those you know and like, and move on from there.

☐ Brandy
☐ Champagne or sparkling wine
☐ Dubonnet
☐ Gin
☐ Rum, dark
☐ Rum, white
☐ Scotch whisky
☐ Sherry, dry
☐ Vermouth, dry
☐ Vermouth, red (sweet)
☐ Vodka
☐ Wine

The drinks in the next list occur in a much smaller number of the recipes, so don't buy them until you are sure you are going to use them. If you are feeling adventurous, you can try creating your own cocktails by substituting or omitting any of these more unusual ingredients.

☐ Amaretto
☐ Aniseed liqueur such as kummel
☐ Apricot brandy
☐ Benedictine
☐ Bourbon

- ☐ Calvados or apple brandy
- ☐ Campari
- ☐ Canadian Club whisky
- ☐ Chartreuse, green and yellow
- ☐ Cherry brandy
- ☐ Coffee cream liqueur such as Bailey's
- ☐ Coffee liqueur such as Tia Maria or Kahlua
- ☐ Curaçao, brown, blue and orange
- ☐ Drambuie
- ☐ Dubonnet
- ☐ Fruit liqueurs – orange, such as Cointreau, plus blackcurrant (crème de cassis), lemon (sirop de citron), melon, raspberry, strawberry (fraisette)
- ☐ Galliano
- ☐ Irish whiskey
- ☐ Lillet
- ☐ Peach schnapps
- ☐ Peppermint liqueur or crème de menthe
- ☐ Pernod
- ☐ Port
- ☐ Sherry, sweet
- ☐ Sloe gin
- ☐ Southern Comfort
- ☐ Triple sec

Other ingredients

All these items are only needed in small quantities. Fortunately, they will last almost for ever if you keep them in a cool, dark cupboard.

- ☐ Angostura bitters
- ☐ Cinnamon sticks
- ☐ Crème de cassis
- ☐ Grenadine
- ☐ Maple syrup
- ☐ Maraschino
- ☐ Orange bitters
- ☐ Orange syrup
- ☐ Peach bitters
- ☐ Salt
- ☐ Sugar syrup. You can use caster (superfine) sugar in cocktails, but sugar syrup gives a much better result. It is available in bottles, but it is easy to make your own. Heat 60 ml/4 tbsp of water and 60 ml/4 tbsp of caster sugar in a pan, stirring gently, until dissolved. Bring to the boil, then boil without stirring for 1 minute. Store in a sterilised bottle in the fridge. It will keep for up to 2 months.
- ☐ Tabasco sauce
- ☐ Worcestershire sauce

Fresh ingredients

A few cocktails make use of fresh ingredients. Citrus fruit juices should be freshly squeezed, if possible, but bottled lemon juice and cartons of fresh orange juice can be used instead. However, there is no substitute for fresh lime juice, so keep a few limes handy! The items on this list must obviously be bought in as required and stored in the fridge.

- ☐ Coconut cream
- ☐ Double cream
- ☐ Eggs
- ☐ Fruit
- ☐ Fruit juices, such as orange, pineapple and tomato
- ☐ Milk, full-cream

Soft drinks and mixers

Start with a few favourites and build up your collection. Do remember that bottles of carbonated drinks such as soda water will go flat quite quickly, so don't buy them in large quantities unless you're having a party.

- ☐ Bitter lemon
- ☐ Ginger ale
- ☐ Soda water
- ☐ Sweet and sour mixer

Garnishes

Garnishes add both flavour and fun, especially if you include a decorative umbrella or a plastic butterfly! Whole small items, such as cherries and olives, should be placed on cocktail sticks (toothpicks), whilst slices of orange, lemon, etc. can be hung over the edge of the glass. You can also add a straw, short or long, to suit the drink.

Many cocktails specify particular garnishes – such as the olive in a dry Martini – but you may like to experiment with your own choice to complement the flavours and colours of your drinks.

- ☐ Chocolate – keep a bar ready for grating over sweet drinks
- ☐ Cocktail cherries
- ☐ Cocktail onions
- ☐ Mint leaves
- ☐ Nutmeg – this is best freshly grated
- ☐ Olives – green are more commonly used than black in cocktails
- ☐ Slices and wedges of lemon, orange or lime
- ☐ Slices of apple, cucumber, etc.
- ☐ Twists of citrus rind. Use a potato peeler to pare thin strips 5 cm/2 in long from lemon, orange or lime, taking care to avoid any of the white pith.

These are the most commonly used garnishes, but there are many more, from tiny strawberries to celery sticks!

Ice

For most cocktails, you will need plenty of whole ice cubes or broken or crushed ice. If you like clear ice cubes, use purified drinking water, which you can buy from pharmacists. If a recipe calls for whole ice cubes, this means standard 2.5 cm/1 in ice cubes but you can, of course, buy moulds to make ice into everything from pink elephants to footballs.

To make broken ice, coarsely chop the cubes to about one-third of their size. To make crushed ice, process the broken ice in a blender, but only do this immediately before you use it – crushed ice melts very quickly.

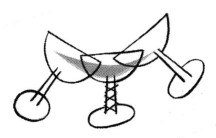

Cocktail Bar Equipment

Fancy cocktail-making gismos make great Christmas gifts for people who have everything, but you don't really need them to try your hand at mixing and serving cocktails. Once you get serious and start making cocktails regularly, take a glance through this list of things to put on your birthday list – and in the meantime, you can use any glasses, jugs or bottles that come to hand.

Glasses

One of the most important elements of serving cocktails is presentation, and so every cocktail has its own style, shape and size of glass. Some of these are quite obscure (when did you last use a pousse café glass?) so in this book you will find only five types of glass.

☐ Cocktail glasses holding about 75 ml/2½ fl oz.

☐ Wine glasses holding about 150 ml/¼ pt/⅔ cup. They may be used instead of champagne flutes, saucers and sundae glasses.

☐ Tall glasses holding about 300 ml/½ pt/1¼ cups. Use them for cocktails that call for highball or Collins glasses.

☐ Whisky tumblers holding about 250 ml/8 fl oz/1 cup.

☐ Goblets holding about 350 ml/12 fl oz/1⅓ cups.

Always use sparkling clean, polished glasses for your cocktails, and make sure they are cold so that they do not warm the drinks. If you don't have exactly the correct glass, try to use one that is as close as possible to the one recommended.

Cocktail shaker

This is one piece of special equipment that is really essential. Made up of two tightly fitting metal containers, it's perfectly designed for shaking cocktails without everything leaking out and spraying round the room. One part has a built-in strainer. For last-minute emergencies, you could use a thermos flask and strain the drink through a tea-strainer.

Cocktail measure

In order to make authentic cocktails, you do need to measure the ingredients. You can buy special calibrated cocktail measures, which look the part, but in practice any measuring jug or cup will suffice. All the recipes in this book use a standard cocktail measure, which is equivalent to about 25 ml, and each recipe makes up the quantity required for a drink for one person. The actual size of the measure is not really important – you can change the quantities to make as much or as little as you wish. However, it is essential that you use the ingredients in the correct proportions.

Mixing glass and spoon

Cocktails that do not require shaking are mixed in a container before being poured into the glass. A large glass tumbler is ideal for this. You will also need a long-handled spoon – like the ones you use for eating ice cream out of tall glasses – for stirring the mixture.

Other utensils

Many of the other items you need for mixing cocktails will be found in your kitchen drawer. The last few on the list overleaf are definitely for the real enthusiast, however, and may have to be bought specially.

- ☐ Small strainer
- ☐ Lemon squeezer
- ☐ Corkscrew
- ☐ Bottle opener
- ☐ Nutmeg grater
- ☐ Fruit knife
- ☐ Straws
- ☐ Cocktail sticks (toothpicks)
- ☐ Ice bucket
- ☐ Ice tongs
- ☐ Muddler – a small tool for crushing sugar and bruising fruit or herbs
- ☐ Ice pick
- ☐ Decanter bottles with stoppers for serving drinks in dashes

Cocktail Terms and Techniques

You can impress your friends by knowing the right terminology and methods for preparing your cocktails. The techniques themselves are straightforward, so the real trick is to perform them with style.

To stir a cocktail

This method is used for cocktails with clear ingredients so that they are mixed and chilled but retain their sparkling clarity.

- ☐ Put a glassful of broken ice into a mixing glass.
- ☐ Add the measured ingredients.
- ☐ Mix briskly and evenly for about 20 seconds with a long-handled spoon.
- ☐ Pour the liquid and ice into a chilled serving glass.

To stir and strain a cocktail

Some clear ingredients are stirred and strained.

- ☐ Half-fill a mixing glass with whole ice cubes.
- ☐ Add the measured ingredients.
- ☐ Mix briskly and evenly for about 20 seconds with a long-handled spoon.
- ☐ Strain the liquid into a chilled serving glass.

To shake a cocktail

The object here is to combine the ingredients thoroughly and cool them without diluting them by over-melting the ice.

☐ Put a glassful of broken ice into a cocktail shaker.

☐ Add the measured ingredients.

☐ Replace the lid firmly, then hold the shaker in both hands and shake briskly and thoroughly until the ingredients are well mixed and cooled.

☐ Pour the liquid and ice into a chilled serving glass.

To shake and strain a cocktail

Cocktails that are shaken and strained are made with whole ice cubes.

☐ Half-fill the cocktail shaker with whole ice cubes.

☐ Add the measured ingredients.

☐ Replace the lid firmly, then hold the shaker in both hands and shake briskly and thoroughly until the ingredients are well mixed and cooled.

☐ Strain into a chilled serving glass.

To add a dash

A 'dash' is a few drops of a bottled ingredient such as angostura bitters. It amounts to about ⅓ of a teaspoon. To add a dash to a drink, shake the upturned bottle once (or twice, according to taste) into the liquid in the glass.

To add a twist of citrus rind

Prepare the twist by paring a strip of rind off the fruit, using a potato peeler (be careful to avoid the white pith). Twist and squeeze the strip of citrus rind over the drink to release the flavour of the essential oil, then add the twist to the drink.

To frost a glass

Frosting glasses makes them look very impressive and it couldn't be simpler. Just chill the glasses in the fridge or freezer until a cold mist forms and freezes on the outside. Keep in the fridge until ready for use.

To coat the rim of a glass

Simply moisten the rim of the glass with water or lemon juice, then dip it into sugar or salt to coat the rim.

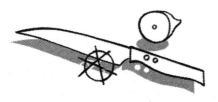

Gin Cocktails

A true essential in any cocktail cabinet, gin makes cocktails that can be anything from the super-sophisticated to the fun and frivolous.

Alexander

2 measures of gin
1 measure of double (heavy) cream
1 measure of white crème de cacao or chocolate-flavoured
liqueur
whole ice cubes
freshly grated nutmeg

Half-fill a cocktail shaker with whole ice cubes, add the measured ingredients and shake. Strain into a chilled cocktail glass and sprinkle with grated nutmeg.

Arizona Cooler

1 measure of gin
1 measure of cranberry juice
1 measure of grapefruit juice
whole ice cubes
soda water
a twist of lemon rind

Half-fill a tall glass with whole ice cubes, then add the measured ingredients. Top up with soda water, stir and add a twist of lemon rind.

Bennett

2 measures of gin
1 measure of lime juice
a dash of angostura bitters
whole ice cubes

Half-fill a cocktail shaker with whole ice cubes, then add the measured ingredients and the bitters. Shake, then strain into a chilled cocktail glass.

Bulldog Cooler

2 measures of gin
½ measure of orange juice
2 dashes of sugar syrup
whole ice cubes
ginger ale
a twist of orange rind

Put two or three whole ice cubes into a tall glass, add the measured ingredients and syrup and top up with ginger ale. Stir well and add a twist of orange rind.

Dry Martini

See photograph on page 65.

2 measures of gin
1 measure of dry vermouth
a dash of orange bitters
whole ice cubes
a twist of lemon rind or a slice of lemon

Half-fill a mixing glass with whole ice cubes. Add the measured ingredients and bitters, then stir. Strain into a chilled cocktail glass and add a twist of lemon rind or slice of lemon.

Gibson

2½ measures of gin
½ measure of dry vermouth
whole ice cubes
a cocktail onion

Half-fill a mixing glass with whole ice cubes. Add the measured ingredients, then stir. Strain into a chilled cocktail glass and garnish with a cocktail onion.

Gimlet

1½ measures of gin
½ measure of lime cordial
whole ice cubes
soda water
a wedge of lime

Half-fill a mixing glass with whole ice cubes. Add the measured ingredients, then stir. Strain into a chilled whisky tumbler, top up with soda water and garnish with a wedge of lime.

Gin Crusta

See photograph on page 104.

2 measures of gin
1 measure of lemon juice
1 teaspoon of sugar syrup
1 teaspoon of maraschino or pineapple syrup
a dash of angostura bitters
a dash of orange bitters
whole ice cubes
a little caster (superfine) sugar
lemon juice

Moisten the edges of a small wine glass with lemon juice, then dip the rim in caster sugar. Half-fill a cocktail shaker with whole ice cubes, add the measured ingredients and the bitters and shake. Strain into the prepared glass.

Gin Daisy

2 measures of gin
2 measures of lemon juice
½ measure of grenadine
whole ice cubes
broken ice
soda water
a twist of lemon rind and slices of fresh fruit

Half-fill a cocktail shaker with whole ice cubes, add the measured ingredients and shake. Strain into a chilled whisky tumbler half-filled with broken ice, then top up with soda water. Add a twist of lemon rind and garnish with slices of fresh fruit.

Gin and Lime Fizz

See photograph on page 66.

2 measures of gin
1 measure of lime juice
1 teaspoon of sugar syrup
1 egg white
soda water
whole ice cubes

Half-fill a cocktail shaker with whole ice cubes, add the measured ingredients and egg white and shake. Strain into a chilled tall glass and top up with soda water to taste. Add a few ice cubes and serve with straws.

Gin Sling

2 measures of gin
1 measure of lemon juice
2 teaspoons of sugar syrup
whole ice cubes
water or soda water
a twist of lemon rind and grated nutmeg (optional)

Place a few whole ice cubes in a whisky tumbler. Add the measured ingredients and fill up with water or soda water. Add a twist of lemon rind and sprinkle with a little nutmeg, if liked, and serve with a straw.

Green Dragon

See photograph on page 104.

1½ measures of gin
¾ measure of crème de menthe
½ measure of kummel or peppermint-flavoured liqueur
½ measure of lemon juice
2 dashes of peach or orange bitters
whole ice cubes

Half-fill a cocktail shaker with whole ice cubes, add the measured ingredients and the bitters and shake. Strain into a chilled cocktail glass.

Hawaiian

1½ measures of gin
1½ measures of orange juice
a dash of Cointreau
whole ice cubes
a slice of orange

Half-fill a cocktail shaker with whole ice cubes, add the measured ingredients and the Cointreau and shake. Strain into a chilled cocktail glass and garnish with a slice of orange.

High Velocity

2 measures of gin
1 measure of red vermouth
whole ice cubes
a slice of orange

Half-fill a cocktail shaker with whole ice cubes, add all the ingredients and shake. Strain into a chilled cocktail glass and garnish with a slice of orange.

Inca

¾ measure of gin
¾ measure of dry sherry
¾ measure of dry vermouth
¾ measure of red vermouth
a dash of orange syrup
a dash of orange bitters
broken ice
a twist of lemon rind

Half-fill a mixing glass with broken ice, add all the ingredients and stir. Strain into a chilled cocktail glass and add a twist of lemon rind.

John Collins

2 measures of gin
1 measure of lemon or lime juice
1 teaspoon of sugar syrup
whole ice cubes
broken ice
soda water
slices of lemon or lime

Half-fill a cocktail shaker with whole ice cubes, add the measured ingredients and shake. Strain into a chilled tall glass half-filled with broken ice, top up with soda water and garnish with slices of lemon or lime. Serve with straws.

Knickerbocker

1½ measures of gin
¾ measure of dry vermouth
a dash of red vermouth
broken ice
a twist of lemon rind
a cocktail cherry

Half-fill a mixing glass with broken ice, add the gin and vermouths and stir well. Strain into a chilled cocktail glass, add a twist of lemon rind and garnish with a cocktail cherry.

London

See photograph on page 101.

1 measure of gin
a dash of orange bitters
a dash of sugar syrup
a dash of Pernod
broken ice
green olives
a piece of lemon

Half-fill a mixing glass with broken ice, add the ingredients and stir. Strain into a chilled cocktail glass and garnish with green olives and a small piece of lemon.

Luigi

1½ measures of gin
1½ measures of dry vermouth
1 teaspoon of grenadine
½ teaspoon of Cointreau
juice of half a tangerine
whole ice cubes
a twist of lemon rind
a slice of orange and a cocktail cherry

Half-fill a cocktail shaker with whole ice cubes, add the measured ingredients and the tangerine juice and shake. Strain into a chilled cocktail glass, add a twist of lemon rind and garnish with a slice of orange and a cocktail cherry.

Mississippi Mule

2 measures of gin
½ measure of crème de cassis
½ measure of lemon juice
whole ice cubes

Half-fill a cocktail shaker with whole ice cubes, add the measured ingredients and shake. Strain into a chilled cocktail glass.

Monkey Gland

2 measures of gin
1 measure of orange juice
1 teaspoon of Pernod
2 teaspoon of grenadine
whole ice cubes
a slice of orange
a cocktail cherry

Half-fill a cocktail shaker with whole ice cubes, add the measured ingredients and shake. Strain into a chilled cocktail glass and garnish with a slice of orange wrapped round a cocktail cherry.

Negroni

1 measure of gin
1 measure of red vermouth
1 measure of Campari
broken ice
½ slice of orange

Put all the ingredients into a mixing glass and stir, then strain into a chilled whisky tumbler three-quarters full of broken ice. Garnish with a half slice of orange.

Orange Blossom

See photograph on page 65.

1½ measures of gin
1½ measures of red vermouth
1½ measures of orange juice
whole ice cubes
a slice of orange

Half-fill a cocktail shaker with whole ice cubes, add the measured ingredients and shake. Strain into a chilled cocktail glass and garnish with a slice of orange.

Paradise

1 measure of gin
1 measure of apricot brandy
1 measure of orange juice
whole ice cubes
a white flower blossom
a cocktail cherry

Half-fill a cocktail shaker with whole ice cubes, add the measured ingredients and shake. Strain into a chilled cocktail glass and garnish with a white flower – an orchid if you can get one! – and a cocktail cherry.

Parisian

1 measure of gin
1 measure of crème de cassis
1 measure of dry vermouth
broken ice

Half-fill a mixing glass with broken ice, add the measured ingredients and stir. Strain into a chilled cocktail glass.

Pegu Club

See photograph on page 66.

2 measures of gin
1 measure of Cointreau
a dash of angostura bitters
a dash of lime juice
a dash of orange bitters
broken ice
a slice of orange

Half-fill a mixing glass with broken ice, add all the ingredients and stir. Strain into a chilled cocktail glass and garnish with a slice of orange.

Perfect

1½ measures of gin
½ measure of red vermouth
½ measure of dry vermouth
a dash of orange bitters
crushed ice
an olive

Half-fill a chilled tall glass with crushed ice, then pour over all the ingredients and garnish with an olive.

Pink Gin

1–2 dashes of angostura bitters
2 measures of gin
iced water

Shake the bitters into a chilled cocktail glass and roll around to coat the sides. Add the gin and top up with iced water.

Pink Lady

1½ measures of gin
1 measure of egg white
½ measure of grenadine
whole ice cubes

Half-fill a cocktail shaker with whole ice cubes, add the ingredients and shake, then strain into a chilled cocktail glass.

Polo

See photograph on page 65.

1 measure of gin
1 measure of dry vermouth
1 measure of red vermouth
2 teaspoons of lemon or lime juice
whole ice cubes
a slice of lemon

Half-fill a cocktail shaker with whole ice cubes, add the measured ingredients and shake. Strain into a chilled cocktail glass and garnish with a slice of lemon.

Prince's Smile

1½ measures of gin
¾ measure of calvados
¾ measure of apricot brandy
a dash of lemon juice
whole ice cubes
a slice of lemon

Half-fill a cocktail shaker with whole ice cubes, add the measured ingredients and lemon juice and shake. Strain into a chilled cocktail glass and garnish with a slice of lemon.

RAC

See photograph on page 65.

1½ measures of gin
¾ measure of dry vermouth
¾ measure of red vermouth
a dash of grenadine
a dash of orange bitters
broken ice
a twist of orange rind
a cocktail cherry

Half-fill a mixing glass with broken ice and add the measured ingredients, grenadine and bitters. Stir well, then strain into a chilled cocktail glass, add a twist of orange rind and garnish with a cocktail cherry.

Royal

2 measures of gin
1 measure of Dubonnet
a dash of orange bitters
a dash of angostura bitters
broken ice
a twist of lemon rind
a cocktail cherry

Half-fill a mixing glass with broken ice, add the measured ingredients and the bitters and stir well. Strain into a chilled cocktail glass, add a twist of lemon rind and garnish with a cocktail cherry.

Royal Fizz

See photograph on page 65.

2 measures of gin
½ egg, beaten
juice of ½ lemon
½ teaspoon of sugar syrup or grenadine
whole ice cubes
broken ice
soda water

Half-fill a cocktail shaker with whole ice cubes, add the measured ingredients and shake. Strain into a chilled tall glass half-filled with broken ice and top up with soda water.

Sandmartin

1½ measures of gin
1½ measures of red vermouth
1 teaspoon of green chartreuse (optional)
broken ice
a twist of lemon rind

Half-fill a mixing glass with broken ice, add the measured ingredients and stir well. Strain into a chilled cocktail glass and add a twist of lemon rind.

Silver Streak

See photograph on page 104.

1 measure of gin
1 measure of kummel or peppermint liqueur
whole ice cubes

Half-fill a cocktail shaker with whole ice cubes, add the measured ingredients and shake. Strain into a chilled cocktail glass.

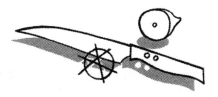

Singapore Sling

See photograph on page 101.

1 measure of gin
1 measure of cherry brandy
½ measure of triple sec or orange-flavoured liqueur
1 measure of lime juice
1 measure of pineapple juice
1 measure of orange juice
¼ measure of grenadine
a dash of angostura bitters
whole ice cubes
broken ice
a slice of pineapple
a cocktail cherry

Half-fill a cocktail shaker with whole ice cubes, then add the measured ingredients and bitters and shake. Half-fill a chilled tall glass with broken ice, then strain in the cocktail and garnish with a slice of pineapple and a cocktail cherry.

Southern Gin

2 measures of gin
2 dashes of Cointreau
2 dashes of orange bitters
whole ice cubes
a twist of lemon rind

Half-fill a cocktail shaker with whole ice cubes, add all the ingredients and shake. Strain into a chilled cocktail glass, then add a twist of lemon rind.

Strawberry Cream Cooler

See photograph on page 67.

1 measure of gin
½ measure of orange juice
1½ measures of double (heavy) cream
3 strawberries
1 teaspoon of caster (superfine) sugar
whole ice cubes
soda water

Blend all the measured ingredients and the strawberries together in a liquidiser for a few seconds, then pour into a chilled tumbler over whole ice cubes and top up with soda water.

Strawberry Dawn

See photograph on page 67.

1 measure of gin
1 measure of coconut cream
3 strawberries
2 scoops of crushed ice

Blend together all the ingredients, including the ice, for a few seconds in a liquidiser, then pour into a chilled cocktail glass.

Tipperary

2 measures of gin
1 measure of red vermouth
1 teaspoon of orange juice
3 dashes of grenadine
2 sprigs of fresh mint
whole ice cubes
a cocktail cherry or a strawberry

Half-fill a cocktail shaker with whole ice cubes, add the measured ingredients with the grenadine and mint, and shake. Strain into a chilled cocktail glass and garnish with a cocktail cherry or a fresh strawberry.

Western Rose

1½ measures of gin
½ measure of dry vermouth
½ measure of apricot brandy
a dash of lemon juice
whole ice cubes

Half-fill a cocktail shaker with whole ice cubes, add the measured ingredients and lemon juice and shake. Strain into a chilled cocktail glass.

White Lady

1 measure of lemon juice
1 measure of Cointreau
2 measures of gin
whole ice cubes
a twist of lemon rind

Half-fill a cocktail shaker with whole ice cubes, add the measured ingredients and shake. Strain into a chilled cocktail glass and add a twist of lemon rind.

Whizz-bang Cooler

See photograph on page 103.

2 measures of gin
a dash of crème de menthe
whole ice cubes
ginger ale
a sprig of mint

Put whole ice cubes into a chilled tall glass. Add the gin and crème de menthe, stir well and top up with ginger ale. Garnish with a sprig of mint.

Vodka Cocktails

For the latest light and stylish cocktails, invest in a bottle of vodka for your cocktail cabinet. Experiment and enjoy!

Alabama Slammer

1 measure of vodka
1 measure of bourbon
1 measure of amaretto
4 measures of orange juice
a dash of grenadine
whole ice cubes
broken ice

Half-fill a cocktail shaker with whole ice cubes, add the measured ingredients and grenadine and shake. Strain into a chilled tall glass half-filled with broken ice.

Balalaika

1 measure of vodka
1 measure of Cointreau
1 measure of lemon juice
whole ice cubes

Half-fill a cocktail shaker with whole ice cubes, add the measured ingredients and shake. Strain into a chilled cocktail glass.

Bellini

1 measure of vodka
1 measure of peach schnapps
1 measure of sugar syrup
1 scoop of crushed ice
2 measures of peach juice
2 canned peach slices
2 measures of champagne or sparkling wine
whole ice cubes

Blend all the ingredients except the champagne or sparkling wine and whole ice cubes in a liquidiser until smooth. Put a few whole ice cubes into a chilled tall glass, pour in the mixture and top up with champagne or sparkling wine.

Black Russian

2 measures of vodka
1 measure of Kalhua or coffee-flavoured liqueur
broken ice
cola (optional)

Half-fill a chilled tall glass with broken ice, add the measured ingredients and stir gently. Top up with cola, if using, and serve with straws.

Bloody Mary

2 measures of vodka
½ teaspoon of lemon juice
2 dashes of Worcestershire sauce
4 drops of Tabasco sauce
a pinch of salt and pepper
whole ice cubes
tomato juice
a short celery stalk with leaves

Place the whole ice cubes in a tall glass and add the measured ingredients, sauces and seasoning. Top up with tomato juice and stir well. Garnish with a celery stalk.

Cape Cod

1 measure of vodka
3 measures of cranberry juice
whole ice cubes
soda water
a twist of lime rind

Half-fill a chilled tall glass with whole ice cubes, pour over the vodka and cranberry juice and top up with soda water to taste. Garnish with a twist of lime rind.

Greased Lightning

2 measures of vodka
1 measure of triple sec or orange-flavoured liqueur
1 measure of lime juice
whole ice cubes

Half-fill a cocktail shaker with whole ice cubes, add the measured ingredients and shake. Strain into a chilled cocktail glass.

Green Eyes

1½ measures of vodka
1 measure of blue curaçao or orange-flavoured liqueur
3 measures of orange juice
whole ice cubes
broken ice
a twist of lime rind

Half-fill a cocktail shaker with whole ice cubes, add the measured ingredients and shake. Strain into a chilled tall glass half-filled with broken ice and add a twist of lime rind.

Harvey Wallbanger

2 measures of vodka
4 measures of orange juice
¾ measure of Galliano or aniseed liqueur
whole ice cubes
broken ice
a slice of orange

Half-fill a cocktail shaker with whole ice cubes, add the vodka and orange juice and shake. Strain into a chilled tall glass half-filled with broken ice. Sprinkle with the Galliano, garnish with a slice of orange and serve with a straw.

Japanese Slipper

1½ measures of vodka
1 measure of melon liqueur
½ measure of lemon juice
whole ice cubes
a slice of lemon

Half-fill a cocktail shaker with whole ice cubes, add the measured ingredients and shake. Strain into a chilled cocktail glass and garnish with a slice of lemon.

Kamikaze

2 measures of vodka
1 measure of triple sec or orange liqueur
1 measure of lime juice
whole ice cubes

Half-fill a cocktail shaker with whole ice cubes, add the measured ingredients and shake. Strain into a chilled whisky tumbler.

Katinka

2 measures of vodka
1 measure of apricot brandy
½ measure of lime juice
whole ice cubes
crushed ice
a sprig of mint

Half-fill a cocktail shaker with whole ice cubes, add the measured ingredients and shake. Strain into a chilled wine glass over a little crushed ice and garnish with a sprig of mint.

Lemon Drop

2 measures of vodka
1 measure of triple sec or orange liqueur
1 measure of lemon juice
1 measure of sugar syrup
whole ice cubes

Half-fill a cocktail shaker with whole ice cubes, add the measured ingredients and shake. Strain into a chilled whisky tumbler.

Long Island Iced Tea

1 measure of vodka
1 measure of gin
1 measure of white rum
½ measure of triple sec or orange liqueur
½ measure of sweet and sour mixer
whole ice cubes
cola
a twist of lemon rind

Half-fill a cocktail shaker with whole ice cubes, add the measured ingredients and shake. Strain into a chilled tall glass half-filled with ice cubes, then top up with cola and garnish with a twist of lemon rind.

Melon Ball

1½ measures of vodka
1½ measures of melon or other fruit liqueur
½ measure of orange juice
whole ice cubes
a melon ball
a slice of lime

Half-fill a cocktail shaker with whole ice cubes, add the measured ingredients and shake. Strain into a chilled tall glass, garnish with a melon ball and a slice of lime and serve with a straw.

Moscow Mule

1½ measures of vodka
¾ measure of lime juice
whole ice cubes
ginger ale
a wedge of lime

Half-fill a chilled tall glass with ice cubes, then pour over the measured ingredients and top up with ginger ale. Garnish with a wedge of lime and serve with straws.

Salty Dog

1 measure of vodka
4 measures of grapefruit juice
broken ice
salt

Moisten the edge of a chilled tall glass and press into a dish of salt. Half-fill the glass with broken ice, then pour in the measured ingredients.

Screwdriver

2 measures of vodka
4 measures of orange juice
whole ice cubes
a slice of orange
a cocktail cherry

Half-fill a whisky tumbler with whole ice cubes, then add the measured ingredients. Garnish with a slice of orange and a cocktail cherry.

Sea Breeze

2 measures of vodka
2 measures of cranberry juice
2 measures of grapefruit juice
whole ice cubes

Half-fill a chilled tall glass with whole ice cubes, then pour over the ingredients.

Sex on the Beach

1 measure of vodka
1 measure of melon liqueur
1 measure of raspberry liqueur
2 measures of pineapple juice
2 measures of cranberry juice
whole ice cubes

Half-fill a cocktail shaker with whole ice cubes, add the measured ingredients and shake. Strain into a chilled tall glass half-filled with ice cubes.

Slow Comfortable Screw

1 measure of vodka
¾ measure of Southern Comfort
¾ measure of sloe gin
5 measures of orange juice
whole ice cubes
broken ice
a cocktail cherry

Half-fill a cocktail shaker with whole ice cubes, add the measured ingredients and shake. Strain into a chilled tall glass over broken ice, garnish with a cocktail cherry and serve with straws.

SW1

1 measure of vodka
1 measure of Campari
1 measure of orange juice
1 egg white
whole ice cubes

Half-fill a cocktail shaker with whole ice cubes, then add the measured ingredients and egg white and shake. Strain into a chilled cocktail glass and garnish with a cocktail cherry.

Vodka Mist

2 measures of vodka
crushed ice
a twist of lime

Half-fill a cocktail shaker with crushed ice, then add the vodka and shake briefly. Pour, unstrained, into a chilled wine glass and add a twist of lime.

Vodka Rickey

2 measures of vodka
½ lime
4 measures of soda water
whole ice cubes

Half-fill a chilled tall glass with ice cubes, then squeeze the lime juice directly into the glass and add the squeezed lime shell. Pour over the vodka and mix together, then top up with soda water.

Vodka Sour

1 measure of vodka
1 measure of triple sec or orange liqueur
1 measure of lemon juice
1 teaspoon of sugar syrup
whole ice cubes
broken ice
a twist of lemon rind
a cocktail cherry

Half-fill a cocktail shaker with whole ice cubes, add the measured ingredients and shake. Strain into a chilled whisky tumbler filled with broken ice, then garnish with a twist of lemon rind and a cocktail cherry.

Vodkatini

2 measures of vodka
1 measure of dry vermouth
broken ice
a twist of lemon rind

Half-fill a mixing glass with broken ice, add the measured ingredients and stir well. Pour into a chilled cocktail glass and add a twist of lemon rind.

White Russian

1 measure of vodka
1 measure of coffee liqueur
1 measure of double (heavy) cream
broken ice

Half-fill a chilled tall glass with broken ice. Pour over the vodka and coffee liqueur, then top with the cream.

Vodka Cocktails

See photograph on page 65.

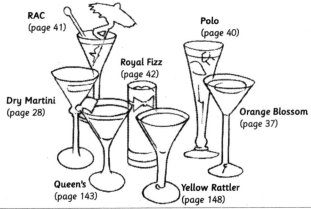

RAC
(page 41)

Polo
(page 40)

Royal Fizz
(page 42)

Dry Martini
(page 28)

Orange Blossom
(page 37)

Queen's
(page 143)

Yellow Rattler
(page 148)

Canadian Club
(page 83)

Oppenheim
(page 75)

Brandy Vermouth
(page 95)

Whisky Sour
(page 81)

Fruit Wine
Cocktail
(page 156)

Pegu Club
(page 38)

Gin and
Lime Fizz
(page 30)

See photograph on page 66.

See photograph on page 67.

Bloodhound
(page 135)

Margarita
(page 120)

American Beauty
(page 90)

Brandy Julep
(page 93)

Strawberry Dawn
(page 46)

Tequila
Sunrise
(page 122)

Strawberry
Cream Cooler
(page 45)

Cuba Libra
(page 115)

Piña Colada
(page 116)

Bacardi Crusta
(page 113)

Spring
Shake-up
(page 118)

Scorpion
(page 117)

Casablanca
(page 115)

Rum Cooler
(page 110)

See photograph on page 68.

Whisky, Whiskey and Bourbon Cocktails

Wicked and warming for those cold winter nights, whisky cocktails should be made with a good blended malt – single malts are best served straight. Canadian Club whisky is lighter than Scotch and smoother than bourbon.

Blood and Sand

See photograph on page 101.

¾ measure of Scotch whisky
¾ measure of red vermouth
¾ cherry brandy
¾ measure of orange juice
broken ice
a cocktail cherry
a slice of lemon

Half-fill a mixing glass with broken ice, add the measured ingredients and stir well. Strain into a chilled cocktail glass and garnish with a cocktail cherry and a slice of lemon.

Bobby Burns

1½ measures of Scotch whisky
1½ measures of red vermouth
1 teaspoon of Benedictine or brandy
broken ice
a cocktail cherry

Half-fill a mixing glass with broken ice, add the measured ingredients and stir well. Strain into a chilled cocktail glass and garnish with a cocktail cherry.

Crow

1 measure of Scotch whisky
2 measures of lemon juice
a dash of grenadine
broken ice

Half-fill a mixing glass with broken ice, add the measured ingredients and the grenadine and stir well. Strain into a chilled cocktail glass.

Hoots Mon

1½ measures of Scotch whisky
¾ measure of red vermouth
¾ measure of Dubonnet
broken ice

Half-fill a mixing glass with broken ice, add the measured ingredients and stir well. Strain into a chilled cocktail glass.

Hot Scotch

2 measures of Scotch whisky
¾ measure of lemon juice
1 teaspoon of caster (superfine) sugar
1 cinnamon stick
boiling water
a wedge of lemon

Put the measured ingredients and the cinnamon in a whisky tumbler, top up with boiling water and stir well to dissolve the sugar. Garnish with a wedge of lemon.

Mickie Walker

2 measures of Scotch whisky
¾ measure of red vermouth
a dash of lemon juice
a dash of grenadine
whole ice cubes

Half-fill a cocktail shaker with whole ice cubes, add the measured ingredients, lemon juice and grenadine, and shake. Strain into a chilled cocktail glass.

Oppenheim

See photograph on page 66.

1½ measures of Scotch whisky
¾ measure of red vermouth
¾ measure of grenadine
broken ice

Half-fill a mixing glass with broken ice, add the measured ingredients and stir. Strain into a chilled cocktail glass.

Rob Roy

See photograph on page 103.

2 measures of Scotch whisky
1 measure of red vermouth
a dash of angostura bitters
broken ice
a cocktail cherry

Half-fill a mixing glass with broken ice, add the measured ingredients and bitters and stir. Strain into a chilled cocktail glass and garnish with a cocktail cherry.

Rusty Nail

2 measures of Scotch whisky
1 measure of Drambuie
whole ice cubes

Put two or three whole ice cubes in a chilled whisky tumbler and pour the measured ingredients over.

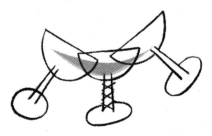

Scotch Mist

2 measures of Scotch whisky
crushed ice
a twist of lemon rind

Put a glassful of crushed ice into a cocktail shaker, add the Scotch and shake briefly, then pour, unstrained, into a chilled whisky tumbler. Add a twist of lemon rind and serve with a straw.

Wembley

1 measure of Scotch whisky
1 measure of dry vermouth
1 measure of pineapple juice
whole ice cubes
broken ice

Half-fill a cocktail shaker with whole ice cubes, add the measured ingredients and shake. Strain into a chilled whisky tumbler half-filled with broken ice.

Whisky Collins

2 measures of Scotch whisky
1 measure of lemon or lime juice
1 teaspoon of sugar syrup
whole ice cubes
broken ice
soda water
slices of lemon or lime

Half-fill a cocktail shaker with whole ice cubes, add the measured ingredients and shake. Strain into a chilled tall glass half-filled with broken ice and top up with soda water. Garnish with slices of lemon or lime and serve with straws.

Whisky Daisy

2 measures of Scotch whisky
1 measure of lemon juice
1 measure of lime juice
½ measure of orange juice
1 teaspoon of grenadine
a dash of brown curaçao (optional)
whole ice cubes
broken ice
soda water
a twist of lemon rind
slices of fresh fruit

Half-fill a cocktail shaker with whole ice cubes, add the measured ingredients and brown curaçao, if liked, and shake. Strain into a chilled whisky tumbler half-filled with broken ice, then top up with soda water. Add a twist of lemon rind and garnish with slices of fresh fruit.

Whisky Fix

2 measures of Scotch whisky
¾ measure of lemon juice
1 teaspoon of sugar syrup
crushed ice
slices of fresh fruit
cold water

Half-fill a whisky tumbler with crushed ice. Put the measured ingredients into a mixing glass, stir well, then pour into the tumbler. Add a twist of lemon rind and garnish with slices of fruit in season. Top up with water to taste.

Whisky Highball

2½ measures of Scotch whisky
broken ice
soda water or ginger ale
a twist of lemon rind

Put the Scotch in a whisky tumbler three-quarters filled with broken ice. Top up with soda water or ginger ale and add a twist of lemon rind.

Whisky Julep

3 measures of Scotch whisky
sprigs of mint
1 teaspoon of caster (superfine) sugar
a little cold water
crushed ice
slices of lime and fresh fruit

Put four sprigs of mint into a whisky tumbler with the sugar and add just enough water to dissolve the sugar. Crush the mint very gently to extract the flavour, then strain into a chilled tall glass. Add the whisky and stir, while topping up with broken ice. Garnish with sprigs of mint, slices of lime and fresh fruit, and serve with a straw.

Whisky Rickey

½ lime
2 measures of Scotch whisky
whole ice cubes
soda water

Half-fill a whisky tumbler with whole ice cubes. Squeeze the lime juice directly into the glass and add the squeezed lime shell and the whisky. Top up with soda water and stir well.

Whisky Sour

See photograph on page 66.

1 measure of Scotch whisky
1 measure of lemon juice
1 teaspoon of sugar syrup
whole ice cubes
broken ice
soda water (optional)
a slice of lemon

Half-fill a cocktail shaker with whole ice cubes, then add the measured ingredients and shake. Strain into a chilled whisky tumbler or small wine glass half-filled with broken ice, then add a little soda water, if liked, and garnish with a slice of lemon.

Irish Coffee

1–2 measures of Irish whiskey
hot black coffee
sugar, to taste
1–2 measures of double (heavy) cream

Pour the whiskey into a wine glass and add the hot black coffee and sweeten to taste. Pour the cream over the back of a warmed spoon so that it floats on the surface of the coffee. Do not stir.

Paddy

1½ measures of Irish whiskey
1½ measures of red vermouth
1 dash of angostura bitters
broken ice

Half-fill a mixing glass with broken ice, add the measured ingredients and bitters and stir, then strain into a chilled cocktail glass.

Shamrock

1½ measures of Irish whiskey
1½ measures of dry vermouth
3 dashes of green chartreuse
3 dashes of crème de menthe
broken ice

Half-fill a mixing glass with broken ice, add all the ingredients and stir, then strain into a chilled cocktail glass.

Shillelagh

2 measures of Irish whiskey
1 teaspoon of peach schnapps
1 teaspoon of white rum
1 teaspoon of lemon juice
1 teaspoon of sugar syrup
broken ice

Half-fill a cocktail shaker with broken ice, add the measured ingredients and shake. Pour, unstrained, into a chilled whisky tumbler.

Canadian Club

See photograph on page 66.

1 measure of Canadian Club whisky
3 dashes of grenadine
a dash of angostura bitters
broken ice
a cocktail cherry

Half-fill a mixing glass with broken ice, add the measured ingredients, grenadine and bitters, and stir. Strain into a chilled cocktail glass and garnish with a cocktail cherry.

Ink Street

1 measure of Canadian Club whisky
1 measure of orange juice
1 measure of lemon juice
whole ice cubes

Half-fill a cocktail shaker with whole ice cubes, add the measured ingredients and shake. Strain into a chilled cocktail glass.

Orient Express

See photograph on page 102.

1 measure of Canadian Club whisky
1 measure of dry vermouth
1 measure of Drambuie
broken ice
a twist of orange rind

Half-fill a mixing glass with crushed ice, add the measured ingredients and stir. Strain into a cocktail glass and add a twist of orange.

New York

2 measures of Canadian Club whisky
¾ measure of lime juice
½ measure of sugar syrup
1 teaspoon of grenadine
whole ice cubes
broken ice
a twist of orange rind

Half-fill a cocktail shaker with whole ice cubes, add the measured ingredients and shake. Strain into a chilled whisky tumbler half-filled with broken ice, and add a twist of orange rind.

Opening Night

1½ measures of Canadian Club whisky
¾ measure of red vermouth
¾ measure of grenadine
broken ice

Half-fill a mixing glass with broken ice, add the measured ingredients and stir, then strain into a chilled cocktail glass.

Palmer

2 measures of Canadian Club whisky
a dash of angostura bitters
a dash of lemon juice
whole ice cubes
broken ice

Half-fill a cocktail shaker with whole ice cubes, add all the ingredients and shake. Strain into a chilled whisky tumbler half-filled with broken ice.

Algonquin

2 measures of bourbon
1 measure of dry vermouth
1 measure of pineapple juice
whole ice cubes
broken ice

Half-fill a cocktail shaker with whole ice cubes, add the measured ingredients and shake. Strain into a chilled whisky tumbler half-filled with broken ice.

Los Angeles

2 measures of bourbon
½ measure of lemon juice
1 teaspoon of sugar syrup
¼ beaten egg
a dash of red vermouth
whole ice cubes

Half-fill a cocktail shaker with whole ice cubes, add the measured ingredients, egg and vermouth, and shake. Strain into a chilled cocktail glass.

Mountain

1½ measures of bourbon
½ measure of dry vermouth
½ measure of red vermouth
½ measure of lemon juice
1 egg white
whole ice cubes

Half-fill a cocktail shaker with whole ice cubes, add all the ingredients and shake. Strain into a chilled cocktail glass.

Old-fashioned

2 measures of bourbon
1 lump of sugar
2 dashes of angostura bitters
whole ice cubes
a slice of orange
a cocktail cherry

Put the lump of sugar in a whisky tumbler, then add the angostura bitters and leave until soaked into the sugar. Half-fill the tumbler with ice cubes and add the whisky. Stir and garnish with a slice of orange and a cocktail cherry. Serve with a muddler.

Scarlett O'Hara

2 measures of bourbon
1 measure of cranberry juice
½ measure of lime juice
whole ice cubes
a cocktail cherry

Half-fill a cocktail shaker with whole ice cubes, add the measured ingredients and shake. Strain into a chilled cocktail glass and garnish with a cocktail cherry.

Brandy Cocktails

Mellow and aromatic, a good-quality brandy will make great cocktails. Reserve the very best to serve on its own in a brandy goblet after a splendid dinner.

American Beauty

See photograph on page 67.

¾ measure of brandy
¾ measure of dry vermouth
¾ measure of grenadine
¾ measure of orange juice
a dash of crème de menthe
whole ice cubes
a little port
a cocktail cherry
a slice of lemon

Half-fill a cocktail shaker with whole ice cubes, add the measured ingredients and the crème de menthe and shake. Strain into a chilled cocktail glass and pour with a little port on top. Garnish with a cherry and a slice of orange.

Applejack Rabbit

½ measure of calvados or apple brandy
½ measure of maple syrup
¼ measure of lemon juice
¼ measure of orange juice
whole ice cubes

Half-fill a cocktail shaker with whole ice cubes and add the ingredients and shake. Strain into a chilled cocktail glass.

Between the Sheets

1¼ measures of brandy or cognac
1 measure of white rum
½ measure of Cointreau
¾ measure of lemon juice
½ measure of sugar syrup
whole ice cubes

Half-fill a cocktail shaker with whole ice cubes, add the measured ingredients and shake. Strain into a chilled cocktail glass.

Brandy Cobbler

2 measures of brandy
1 teaspoon of sugar syrup
1 teaspoon of brown curaçao
whole ice cubes
slices of orange or lemon

Half-fill a cocktail shaker with whole ice cubes, add the measured ingredients and shake. Strain into a chilled tall glass, garnish with slices of orange or lemon and serve with straws.

Brandy Daisy

2 measures of brandy
2 measures of lemon juice
½ measure of grenadine
whole ice cubes
broken ice
soda water
slices of fresh fruit and a twist of lemon rind

Half-fill a cocktail shaker with whole ice cubes, add the measured ingredients and shake. Strain into a chilled whisky tumbler half-filled with broken ice, then top up with soda water. Add a twist of lemon rind and garnish with slices of fresh fruit.

Brandy Fix

See photograph on page 101.

2 measures of brandy
¾ measure of lemon juice
1 teaspoon of sugar syrup
crushed ice
slices of fresh fruit and a twist of lemon rind
cold water

Half-fill a chilled tall glass with crushed ice, then pour in the measured ingredients. Add a twist of lemon rind and garnish with slices of fruit. Top up with water and serve with straws.

Brandy Gump

2 measures of brandy
2 dashes of grenadine
juice of 1 lemon
whole ice cubes
a twist of lemon rind
a cocktail cherry

Half-fill a cocktail shaker with whole ice cubes, add all the ingredients and shake. Strain into a chilled cocktail glass, add a twist of lemon rind and garnish with a cocktail cherry.

Brandy Julep

See photograph on page 67.

3 measures of brandy
sprigs of mint
1 teaspoon of caster (superfine) sugar
a little cold water
crushed ice
slices of lime and fresh fruit

Put four sprigs of mint into a tall glass with the sugar and add just enough water to dissolve the sugar. Crush the mint very gently to extract the flavour, then strain into a chilled tall glass. Add the brandy and stir, whilst topping up with broken ice. Garnish with more sprigs of mint, slices of lime and fresh fruit.

Brandy Manhattan

2 measures of brandy
1 measure of red vermouth
1 dash of angostura bitters
broken ice
a twist of lemon rind
a cocktail cherry

Half-fill a mixing glass with broken ice, add the measured ingredients and the bitters and stir. Strain into a chilled whisky tumbler half-filled with broken ice, add a twist of lemon rind and garnish with a cocktail cherry.

Brandy Smash

See photograph on page 101.

2 measures of brandy
½ lump of sugar
a little water or soda water
sprigs of mint
whole ice cubes

Dissolve the lump of sugar in a little water or soda water in a cocktail shaker. Add four sprigs of mint and crush lightly with a muddler, then remove them. Half-fill the shaker with ice cubes, put in the brandy and shake well. Strain into a chilled wine glass and garnish with a sprig of mint.

Brandy Sour

1 measure of brandy
1 measure of lemon juice
1 teaspoon of sugar syrup
whole ice cubes
broken ice
soda water (optional)
a twist of lemon rind
a cocktail cherry

Half-fill a cocktail shaker with whole ice cubes, add the measured ingredients and shake. Strain into a chilled whisky tumbler half-filled with broken ice, then add a little soda water, if liked, and garnish with a twist of lemon rind and a cocktail cherry.

Brandy Vermouth

See photograph on page 66.

2 measures of brandy
2 measures of red vermouth
whole ice cubes
a slice of lemon

Half-fill a cocktail shaker with whole ice cubes, add the measured ingredients and shake. Strain into a chilled cocktail glass and garnish with a slice of lemon.

Charles

1½ measures of brandy
1½ measures of red vermouth
a dash of angostura bitters
broken ice

Half-fill a mixing glass with broken ice, add all the ingredients and stir. Strain into a chilled cocktail glass.

Cold Brandy Toddy

2 measures of brandy
1 lump of sugar
a little cold water
1 whole ice cube

Put the sugar into a whisky tumbler and add just enough water to dissolve it. Add a lump of ice and the brandy and stir well.

Cuban

1½ measures of brandy
¾ measure of apricot brandy
¾ measure of lime juice
broken ice

Half-fill a mixing glass with broken ice, add the measured ingredients and stir. Strain into a chilled cocktail glass.

Egg Punch

See photograph on page 104.

3 measures of brandy
1 teaspoon of sugar syrup
1 egg
broken ice
cold full-cream milk
a little freshly grated nutmeg

Half-fill a cocktail shaker with broken ice, add the measured ingredients and the egg and shake. Strain into a chilled tall glass, top up with milk and sprinkle with a little freshly grated nutmeg.

French

1 measure of brandy
1 measure of sweet and sour mixer
whole ice cubes
champagne or sparkling wine
a twist of lemon rind

Half-fill a cocktail shaker with whole ice cubes, add the measured ingredients and shake. Half-fill a chilled tall glass with ice cubes, then strain in the cocktail and top up with champagne or sparkling wine. Garnish with a twist of lemon rind and serve with straws.

Hoop La!

¾ measure of brandy
¾ measure of Cointreau
¾ measure of Lillet
¾ measure of lemon juice
whole ice cubes

Half-fill a cocktail shaker with whole ice cubes, add the measured ingredients and shake. Strain into a chilled cocktail glass.

Rolls Royce

1 measure of brandy
1 measure of Cointreau
1 measure of orange juice
1 egg white
whole ice cubes
a slice of orange

Half-fill a cocktail shaker with whole ice cubes, add the measured ingredients and the egg white and shake. Strain into a chilled cocktail glass and garnish with a slice of orange.

Sidecar

1 measure of brandy
1 measure of Cointreau
1 measure of lemon juice
whole ice cubes
a slice of lemon

Half-fill a cocktail shaker with whole ice cubes, add the measured ingredients and shake. Strain into a chilled cocktail glass and garnish with a slice of lemon.

Three Miler

See photograph on page 102.

2 measures of brandy
1 measure of white rum
a dash of grenadine
a dash of lemon juice
whole ice cubes

Half-fill a cocktail shaker with whole ice cubes, add all the ingredients and shake. Strain into a chilled cocktail glass.

Brandy Cocktails

See photograph on page 101.

Top row, left to right:
Blood and Sand (page 72)
Brandy Fix (page 92)
Singapore Sling (page 44)
Brandy Smash (page 94)

Bottom row, left to right:
Cooperstown (page 138)
London (page 34)
Vanderbilt (page 130)

Top row, left to right:
Port Wine Negus (page 128)
Heart Stirrer (page 157)
Buck's Fizz (page 152)
Vermouth Cassis Highball
(page 147)

Bottom row, left to right:
After Dinner Blues (page 124)
Orient Express (page 84)
Three Miler (page 99)

See photograph on page 102.

See photograph on page 103.

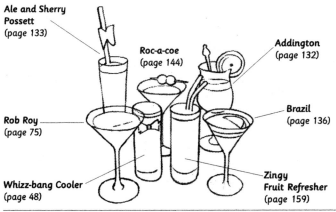

Ale and Sherry Possett
(page 133)

Roc-a-coe
(page 144)

Addington
(page 132)

Rob Roy
(page 75)

Brazil
(page 136)

Whizz-bang Cooler
(page 48)

Zingy Fruit Refresher
(page 159)

Diplomat
(page 139)

Silver Streak
(page 43)

Sunset Cooler
(page 146)

White Wine Cup
(page 159)

Gin Crusta
(page 29)

Green Dragon
(page 31)

Egg Punch
(page 97)

See photograph on page 104.

Rum and Tequila Cocktails

With the heat of Mexico and the Caribbean, bring a little sunshine and excitement into your life and make your own Mardi Gras!

Bone Crusher

½ measure of dark rum
½ measure of gin
½ measure of triple sec or orange liqueur
2 measures of sweet and sour mixer
1 measure of cranberry juice
1 measure of champagne or sparkling wine
crushed ice

Put all the ingredients except the ice in a mixing glass and stir. Half-fill a chilled tall glass with crushed ice, then pour over the ingredients.

Hot Rum Toddy

2 measures of dark rum
½ teaspoon of caster (superfine) sugar
2 dashes of lime juice
hot water
freshly grated nutmeg or ground cinnamon

Dissolve the sugar in a little hot water in a tumbler and add the rum and lime juice. Top up with boiling water and sprinkle with a little grated nutmeg or ground cinnamon.

Jamaica Mule

1½ measures of dark rum
¾ measure of lime juice
whole ice cubes
ginger ale
a twist of lime rind

Half-fill a chilled tall glass with ice cubes, then pour over the measured ingredients and top up with ginger ale. Garnish with a twist of lime rind.

Mai Tai

2 measures of dark rum
1 measure of orange curaçao
1 measure of lime juice
1 measure of pineapple juice
½ measure of grenadine
½ measure of sugar syrup
whole ice cubes
a slice of pineapple
a cocktail cherry

Half-fill a cocktail shaker with whole ice cubes, then add the measured ingredients and shake. Half-fill a chilled tall glass with whole ice cubes, then strain in the cocktail. Garnish with a slice of pineapple and a cocktail cherry.

Planter's

2 measures of dark rum
1 measure of sugar syrup
1 measure of lime juice
broken ice
a slice of orange
a cocktail cherry

Half-fill a mixing glass with broken ice, add the measured ingredients and stir. Strain into a chilled cocktail glass and garnish with a slice of orange and a cocktail cherry.

PS I Love You

1 measure of dark rum
1 measure of coffee liqueur
1 measure of amaretto
½ measure of double (heavy) cream
broken ice

Half-fill a chilled tall glass with broken ice, then pour over the measured ingredients and top up with the cream.

Rum Cooler

See photograph on page 68.

2 measures of dark rum
1 measure of lime juice
1 teaspoon of sugar syrup
whole ice cubes
soda water
a slice of lime

Half-fill a tall glass with whole ice cubes, then add the measured ingredients. Top up with soda water, stir and add a slice of lime.

Rum Punch

2 measures of dark rum
½ measure of lemon juice
2 teaspoons of sugar syrup, grenadine or brown curaçao
whole ice cubes
broken ice
sprigs of mint or slices of fresh fruit

Half-fill a cocktail shaker with whole ice cubes, then add the measured ingredients and shake. Strain into a chilled whisky tumbler half-filled with broken ice and garnish with sprigs of mint or slices of fresh fruit.

Spanish Town

2 measures of dark rum
2 dashes of Cointreau
whole ice cubes
a little freshly grated nutmeg

Half-fill a cocktail shaker with whole ice cubes, add the measured ingredients and shake. Strain into a chilled cocktail glass and garnish with a little freshly grated nutmeg.

Tahitian Itch

1 measure of dark rum
1 measure of bourbon
½ measure of Cointreau
2 measures of pineapple juice
a dash of lime juice
ginger ale
whole ice cubes
a twist of lime rind

Half-fill a chilled tall glass with whole ice cubes, pour over the measured ingredients and the lime juice and top up with ginger ale. Garnish with a twist of lime rind.

Watermelon Cooler

2 measures of dark rum
2 measures of cranberry juice
2 measures of orange juice
1 measure of melon liqueur
whole ice cubes

Half-fill a cocktail shaker with whole ice cubes, add the measured ingredients and shake. Strain into a chilled tall glass half-filled with ice cubes.

Zombie

1 measure of dark rum
1 measure of white rum
⅓ measure of orange curaçao
⅓ measure of apricot liqueur
2 measures of pineapple juice
2 measures of orange juice
½ measure of lemon juice
a dash of sugar syrup
whole ice cubes
a pineapple cube
a cocktail cherry

Half-fill a cocktail shaker with whole ice cubes, add the measured ingredients and syrup and shake. Strain into a chilled tall glass half-filled with ice cubes and garnish with the fruit.

Apple Pie

1½ measures of white rum
1½ measures of red vermouth
2 dashes of apricot brandy
whole ice cubes

Half-fill a cocktail shaker with whole ice cubes, add all the ingredients and shake. Strain into a chilled cocktail glass.

Bacardi Crusta

See photograph on page 68.

2 measures of white rum
1 measure of lemon juice
1 teaspoon of sugar syrup
1 teaspoon of Pernod
a dash of angostura bitters
whole ice cubes
lemon juice
a little caster (superfine) sugar
a twist of orange rind

Moisten the edges of a small wine glass with lemon juice, then dip the rim in caster sugar. Half-fill a cocktail shaker with whole ice cubes, add the measured ingredients and bitters and shake. Strain into the prepared glass and garnish with the orange rind.

Bacardi Special

2 measures of white rum
1 measure of gin
1 measure of lime juice
1 teaspoon of grenadine
whole ice cubes
a cocktail cherry

Half-fill a cocktail shaker with whole ice cubes, add the measured ingredients and shake. Strain into a chilled cocktail glass and garnish with a cocktail cherry.

Blue Hawaiian

1½ measures of white rum
½ measure of dark rum
½ measure of blue curaçao
3 measures of pineapple juice
1 measure of coconut cream
crushed ice
a cocktail cherry

Blend all the ingredients in a liquidiser with some crushed ice, then pour into a chilled wine glass and garnish with a cocktail cherry.

Casablanca

See photograph on page 68.

1 measures of white rum
2 measures of pineapple juice
1 measure of coconut cream
a dash of grenadine
whole ice cubes
a cocktail cherry
a slice of orange
a slice of pineapple

Half-fill a cocktail shaker with whole ice cubes, add the measured ingredients and shake. Strain into a chilled wine glass and garnish with a cocktail cherry and a slice each of orange and pineapple.

Cuba Libre

See photograph on page 68.

2 measures of white rum
juice of ½ lime
broken ice
cola

Half-fill a chilled tall glass with broken ice, then squeeze in the lime juice and add the rum with the squeezed lime shell. Top up with cola to taste.

Daiquiri

2 measures of white rum
⅔ measure of lime juice
1 teaspoon of caster (superfine) sugar
whole ice cubes
a twist of lime rind

Half-fill a cocktail shaker with whole ice cubes, add the measured ingredients and shake. Strain into a chilled cocktail glass and garnish with a twist of lime rind.

Piña Colada

See photograph on page 68.

2 measures of white rum
1½ measures of coconut cream
3 measures of pineapple juice
whole ice cubes
a cocktail cherry
a slice of lemon

Half-fill a cocktail shaker with whole ice cubes, add the measured ingredients and shake. Strain into a chilled goblet. Garnish with a cocktail cherry and a slice of lemon.

Roosevelt

1 measure of white rum
1 measure of gin
1 measure of lemon juice
1 measure of grenadine
whole ice cubes

Half-fill a cocktail shaker with whole ice cubes, add the measured ingredients and shake. Strain into a chilled cocktail glass.

Scorpion

See photograph on page 68.

2 measures of white rum
½ measure of brandy
½ measure of orange juice
a dash of orange bitters
1 teaspoon of caster (superfine) sugar
whole ice cubes
a fresh flower

Half-fill a cocktail shaker with whole ice cubes, add the measured ingredients and bitters and shake. Strain over a little crushed ice in a chilled saucer-shaped glass and garnish with a fresh flower.

Spring Shake-up

See photograph on page 68.

2 measures of white rum
2 measures of pineapple juice
1 measure of Cointreau
a dash of angostura bitters
a dash of grenadine
soda water
whole ice cubes
a cocktail cherry or small strawberry

Half-fill a cocktail shaker with whole ice cubes, add the measured ingredients, bitters and grenadine, and shake. Pour into a tall glass and top up with soda water. Garnish with a cocktail cherry and a strawberry and serve with straws.

Twelve Miles Out

1 measure of white rum
1 measure of calvados or apple brandy
1 measure of lime juice
broken ice
a slice of lemon

Half-fill a mixing glass with broken ice, add the measured ingredients and stir. Strain into a chilled cocktail glass and garnish with a slice of lemon.

XYZ

2 measures of white rum
1 measure of Cointreau
1 measure of lemon juice
whole ice cubes

Half-fill a cocktail shaker with whole ice cubes, add the measured ingredients and shake. Strain into a chilled cocktail glass.

Buttock Clencher

1 measure of tequila
1 measure of gin
2 measures of pineapple juice
2 measures of lemonade
whole ice cubes
a cocktail cherry

Half-fill a cocktail shaker with whole ice cubes, add the tequila, gin and pineapple juice and shake. Strain into a chilled tall glass with more ice, if liked, add the lemonade and garnish with a cocktail cherry.

Margarita

See photograph on page 67.

2 measures of tequila
1 measure of Cointreau
2 measures of lemon juice
whole ice cubes
a thin wedge of lemon
a little salt

Moisten the edge of a chilled cocktail glass with lemon juice and dip into a little salt to coat. Half-fill a cocktail shaker with whole ice cubes, add the measured ingredients and shake. Strain into the prepared glass and garnish with a wedge of lemon.

Peach Margarita

1 measure of tequila
1 measure of peach schnapps
½ measure of triple sec
⅓ ripe peach, peeled and mashed
a little lemon juice
a little caster (superfine) sugar
crushed ice

Moisten the edge of a chilled cocktail glass with lemon juice and dip into a little caster sugar to coat. Blend all the ingredients in a liquidiser with some crushed ice, then pour into the prepared glass.

Pink Cadillac

2 measures of tequila
2 measures of cranberry juice
½ measure of triple sec or orange-flavoured liqueur
a scoop of crushed ice
a slice of lime

Mix the measured ingredients and the ice in a blender until smooth, then pour into a chilled tall glass and garnish with a slice of lime.

Tequila Maria

2 measures of tequila
½ teaspoon of lime juice
2 dashes of Worcestershire sauce
4 drops of Tabasco sauce
a pinch of salt and pepper
whole ice cubes
tomato juice
a twist of lime rind

Place the ice in a tall glass. Add all the ingredients, top up with tomato juice, and stir. Garnish with a twist of lime rind.

Tequila Sunrise

See photograph on page 67.

2 measures of tequila
4 measures of orange juice
½ measure of grenadine
whole ice cubes
a slice of orange (optional)
a cocktail cherry (optional)

Half-fill a cocktail shaker with whole ice cubes, add the measured ingredients and shake. Strain into a chilled tall glass half-filled with ice cubes. Garnish with a slice of orange and a cocktail cherry, if liked.

Liqueur Cocktails

Once you really get bitten by the cocktail bug, you'll want to expand your repertoire. The great thing about liqueurs is that you can often buy half bottles – or even miniatures – if you want to try them out.

After Dinner Blues

See photograph on page 102.

2 measures of blue curaçao
1 measure of double (heavy) cream

Pour the curaçao into a chilled cocktail glass, then gently pour the cream on top of the liqueur over the back of a teaspoon so that it floats on the top. Do not stir.

After Supper

1 measure of Cointreau
1 measure of apricot brandy
4 dashes of lemon juice
whole ice cubes
a slice of lemon

Half-fill a cocktail shaker with whole ice cubes, add the measured ingredients and the lemon juice and shake. Strain into a chilled cocktail glass and garnish with a slice of lemon.

Angel Face

1 measure of apricot brandy
1 measure of calvados or apple brandy
1 measure of gin
whole ice cubes

Half-fill a cocktail shaker with whole ice cubes, add the measured ingredients and shake. Strain into a chilled cocktail glass.

B52

1 measure of Tia Maria or coffee liqueur
1 measure of Bailey's or coffee cream liqueur
1 measure of Cointreau
whole ice cubes

Pour all the ingredients into a chilled whisky tumbler half-filled with whole ice cubes.

Cranberry Cooler

1½ measures of amaretto
3 measures of cranberry juice
1 measure of orange juice
whole ice cubes
a slice of orange
a cocktail cherry

Half-fill a cocktail shaker with whole ice cubes, add the measured ingredients and shake. Strain into a chilled tall glass and garnish with a slice of orange and a cocktail cherry.

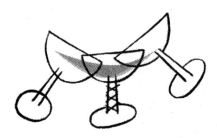

Grasshopper

1 measure of green crème de menthe
1 measure of white crème de cacao or coffee liqueur
1 measure of double (heavy) cream
whole ice cubes

Half-fill a cocktail shaker with whole ice cubes, add the measured ingredients and shake. Strain into a chilled champagne or wine glass and serve with straws.

Johnny Mack

2 measures of sloe gin
1 measure of orange curaçao
3 dashes of Pernod
broken ice

Half-fill a mixing glass with broken ice, add all the ingredients and stir. Strain into a chilled cocktail glass.

Lady Killer

1 measure of Cointreau or orange liqueur
1 measure of gin
½ measure of apricot brandy
2 measures of pineapple juice
2 measures of passion fruit juice
whole ice cubes
a slice of orange

Half-fill a cocktail shaker with whole ice cubes, add the measured ingredients and shake. Strain into a chilled tall glass over ice and garnish with a slice of orange.

Port Wine Negus

See photograph on page 102.

3 measures of port
1 teaspoon of sugar syrup
a dash of brandy
boiling water
a cocktail cherry

Pour the port into a tall wine glass and add the sugar syrup and brandy. Top up with boiling water and garnish with a cocktail cherry.

Porto Fraise

1½ measures of port
½ measure of fraisette (strawberry liqueur)
1 whole ice cube
water or soda water
a small strawberry

Put a whole ice cube into a chilled whisky tumbler and pour in the measured ingredients. Add water or soda water to taste, then stir. Garnish with a strawberry.

Stars and Stripes

1 measure of crème de cassis
1 measure of maraschino
1 measure of green chartreuse

Use a tall, narrow, straight-sided glass, preferably a pousse-café glass. Carefully pour in the crème de cassis, followed by the maraschino, then the green chartreuse, over the back of a spoon. The order is important, as the idea is to keep the liqueurs separate and this can only be done if the densest is put in first. Do not stir.

Vanderbilt

See photograph on page 101.

¾ measure of brandy
¾ measure of cherry brandy
2 dashes of angostura bitters
3 dashes of sugar syrup
broken ice
a twist of lemon rind

Half-fill a mixing glass with broken ice, add the measured ingredients, bitters and syrup, and stir. Strain into a chilled cocktail glass and garnish with a twist of lemon rind.

Velvet Hammer

1½ measures of brandy
1 measure of coffee liqueur
1 measure of double (heavy) cream
whole ice cubes
broken ice
a cocktail cherry

Half-fill a cocktail shaker with whole ice cubes, add the measured ingredients and shake. Strain into a chilled whisky tumbler over broken ice and garnish with a cocktail cherry.

Vermouth and Sherry Cocktails

Often called French and Italian vermouth respectively, dry and red vermouth are versatile bases for a wide variety of cocktails. Add a dry sherry and you have even more scope for enjoyment.

Addington

See photograph on page 103.

1½ measures of dry vermouth
1½ measures of red vermouth
broken ice
soda water
a slice of orange or lemon

Half-fill a mixing glass with broken ice, add the measured ingredients and stir. Strain into a chilled wine glass, top up with soda water and garnish with a slice of orange or lemon.

Adonis

2 measures of dry sherry
1 measure of red vermouth
a dash of orange bitters
broken ice
a twist of orange rind

Half-fill a mixing glass with broken ice, add the measured ingredients and bitters and stir. Strain into a chilled cocktail glass and add a twist of orange rind.

Affinity

1 measure of dry vermouth
1 measure of red vermouth
1 measure of Scotch whisky
a dash of angostura bitters
broken ice
a twist of lemon rind
a cocktail cherry

Half-fill a mixing glass with broken ice, add the measured ingredients and bitters and stir. Strain into a chilled cocktail glass, add a twist of lemon rind and garnish with a cocktail cherry.

Ale and Sherry Possett

See photograph on page 103.

6 measures of milk
1 measure of sherry
1 measure of brown ale
a teaspoon of caster (superfine) sugar
a little freshly grated nutmeg (optional)

Heat the milk until almost boiling. Meanwhile put the sherry, ale and sugar in a mixing glass and stir, then add this to the hot milk and stir again. Pour into a tall glass and sprinkle with a little grated nutmeg, if liked.

Americano

1 measure of red vermouth
1 measure of Campari
broken ice
soda water
a twist of lemon rind

Half-fill a chilled tall glass with broken ice, then pour over the measured ingredients. Top up with soda water and add a twist of lemon rind.

Bamboo

1½ measures of dry sherry
1½ measures of dry vermouth
a dash of orange bitters
broken ice

Half-fill a mixing glass with broken ice, add the measured ingredients and bitters and stir. Strain into a chilled cocktail glass.

Bentley

1½ measures of Dubonnet
1½ measures of calvados or apple brandy
whole ice cubes
a cocktail cherry

Half-fill a cocktail shaker with whole ice cubes, add the measured ingredients and shake. Strain into a chilled cocktail glass and garnish with a cocktail cherry.

Bloodhound

See photograph on page 67.

¾ measure of dry vermouth
¾ measure of red vermouth
1½ measures of gin
3 crushed strawberries
whole ice cubes
a small strawberry

Half-fill a cocktail shaker with whole ice cubes, add the measured ingredients and the crushed strawberries and shake. Strain into a chilled cocktail glass and garnish with a strawberry.

Brazil

See photograph on page 103.

1 measure of dry sherry
1 measure of dry vermouth
a dash of angostura bitters
a dash of Pernod (optional)
broken ice
a slice of lemon

Half-fill a mixing glass with broken ice, add all the ingredients and stir. Strain into a chilled cocktail glass and garnish with a slice of lemon.

BVD

1 measure of dry vermouth
1 measure of white rum
1 measure of gin
whole ice cubes

Half-fill a cocktail shaker with whole ice cubes, add the measured ingredients and shake. Strain into a chilled cocktail glass.

Claridges

1 measure of gin
1 measure of dry vermouth
½ measure of Cointreau
½ measure of apricot brandy
whole ice cubes
a cocktail cherry

Half-fill a cocktail shaker with whole ice cubes, add the measured ingredients and shake. Strain into a chilled cocktail glass and garnish with a cocktail cherry.

Club Cooler

2 measures of red vermouth
1 measure of grenadine
a dash of lemon juice
whole ice cubes
soda water
a twist of lemon rind

Half-fill a tall glass with whole ice cubes and add the measured ingredients and lemon juice. Top up with soda water, stir and add a twist of lemon rind.

Cooperstown

See photograph on page 101.

1 measure of dry vermouth
1 measure of red vermouth
1 measure of gin
sprigs of mint
broken ice
a cocktail cherry

Half-fill a mixing glass with broken ice, add the measured ingredients and a sprig of mint and stir. Strain into a chilled cocktail glass and garnish with a cocktail cherry and an extra sprig of mint, if liked.

Crow's Nest

1 measure of sweet sherry
1 measure of gin
broken ice
a twist of lemon rind

Half-fill a chilled whisky tumbler with broken ice. Pour over the measured ingredients and add a twist of lemon rind.

Diplomat

See photograph on page 104.

2 measures of red vermouth
1 measure of dry vermouth
a dash of maraschino
whole ice cubes
a cocktail cherry

Half-fill the mixing glass with broken ice, add the measured ingredients and the maraschino and stir. Strain into a chilled cocktail glass and garnish with a cocktail cherry.

Dubonnet Citron

3 measures of Dubonnet
1 measure of sirop de citron (lemon liqueur)
1 whole ice cube
still or soda water

Put a whole ice cube into a chilled cocktail glass and pour in the measured ingredients. Add still or soda water to taste, then stir.

Dubonnet Cocktail

1½ measures of Dubonnet
1½ measures of gin
whole ice cubes
a twist of lemon rind

Half-fill a mixing glass with whole ice cubes. Add the measured ingredients, then stir. Strain into a chilled cocktail glass and add a twist of lemon rind.

Easy Action

1 measure of dry vermouth
½ measure of Scotch whisky
½ measure of brandy
1 teaspoon of lemon juice
broken ice
a slice of lemon

Half-fill a cocktail shaker with broken ice, add the measured ingredients and shake. Pour, unstrained, into a chilled whisky tumbler and garnish with a slice of lemon.

Jerez

2 measures of dry sherry
½ measure of brandy
broken ice

Half-fill a chilled whisky tumbler with broken ice and pour the
measured ingredients over.

Lone Tree

1 measure of dry vermouth
1 measure of red vermouth
1 measure of gin
2 dashes of orange bitters
whole ice cubes
a cocktail cherry

Half-fill a cocktail shaker with whole ice cubes, add the
measured ingredients and bitters and shake. Strain into a chilled
cocktail glass and garnish with a cocktail cherry.

One Exciting Night

1 measure of dry vermouth
1 measure of red vermouth
1 measure of gin
a dash of orange juice
whole ice cubes
a twist of lemon rind

Half-fill a cocktail shaker with whole ice cubes, add the measured ingredients and orange juice and shake. Strain into a chilled cocktail glass and add a twist of lemon rind.

Quarter Deck

1 measure of dry sherry
2 measures of dark rum
1 teaspoon of lime juice
broken ice

Half-fill a mixing glass with broken ice, add the measured ingredients and stir. Strain into a chilled cocktail glass.

Queen's

See photograph on page 65.

¾ measure of dry vermouth
¾ measure of red vermouth
1½ measures of gin
broken ice
a small piece of pineapple

Half-fill a mixing glass with broken ice, add the measured ingredients and stir. Pour, unstrained, into a chilled cocktail glass and garnish with a piece of pineapple.

Raymond Hitch

2 measures of red vermouth
juice of ½ orange
a dash of orange bitters
a slice of pineapple, crushed
broken ice

Half-fill a mixing glass with broken ice, add the measured ingredients, bitters and pineapple, and stir. Strain into a chilled cocktail glass.

Roc-a-coe

See photograph on page 103.

1½ measures of dry sherry
1½ measures of gin
broken ice
a cocktail cherry

Half-fill a mixing glass with broken ice, add the measured ingredients and stir. Strain into a chilled cocktail glass and garnish with a cocktail cherry.

Satan's Whiskers

½ measure of dry vermouth
½ measure of red vermouth
½ measure of gin
½ measure of Cointreau
a dash of orange bitters
whole ice cubes

Half-fill a cocktail shaker with whole ice cubes, add the measured ingredients and bitters and shake. Strain into a chilled cocktail glass.

Sherry Cocktail

3 measures of dry sherry
4 dashes of dry vermouth
4 dashes of orange bitters
broken ice

Half-fill a mixing glass with broken ice, add the measured ingredients and stir. Strain into a chilled cocktail glass.

Soul's Kiss

1 measure of dry vermouth
1 measure of Canadian Club whisky
½ measure of Dubonnet
½ measure of orange juice
whole ice cubes
a slice of orange

Half-fill a cocktail shaker with whole ice cubes, add the measured ingredients and shake. Strain into a chilled cocktail glass and garnish with a slice of orange.

Sunset Cooler

See photograph on page 104.

2 measures of Campari
4 measures of orange juice
whole ice cubes
a slice of orange

Half-fill a cocktail shaker with whole ice cubes, add the measured ingredients and shake. Strain into a chilled tall glass and garnish with a slice of orange.

Trocadero

1½ measures of dry vermouth
1½ measures of red vermouth
a dash of grenadine
a dash of orange bitters
broken ice
a twist of lemon rind
a cocktail cherry

Half-fill a mixing glass with broken ice, add the measured ingredients, grenadine and bitters, and stir. Strain into a chilled cocktail glass, add a twist of lemon rind and garnish with a cocktail cherry.

Vermouth Cassis Highball

See photograph on page 102.

1 measure of dry vermouth
1 teaspoon of crème de cassis
soda water or lemonade
a slice of lemon

Pour the measured ingredients into a chilled tall glass, top up with soda water or lemonade and garnish with a slice of lemon.

Washington

2 measures of dry vermouth
1 measure of brandy
2 dashes of sugar syrup
2 dashes of angostura bitters
broken ice

Half-fill a mixing glass with broken ice, add the measured ingredients, syrup and bitters, and stir. Strain into a chilled cocktail glass.

Wyoming Swing

1½ measures of dry vermouth
1½ measures of red vermouth
1 teaspoon of caster (superfine) sugar
½ measure of orange juice
broken ice
soda water

Half-fill a mixing glass with broken ice, add the measured ingredients and stir. Strain into a chilled wine glass and top up with soda water.

Yellow Rattler

See photograph on page 65.

¾ measure of dry vermouth
¾ measure of red vermouth
¾ measure of gin
¾ measure of orange juice
whole ice cubes
a cocktail onion, crushed

Half-fill a cocktail shaker with whole ice cubes, add the measured ingredients and shake. Strain into a chilled cocktail glass and garnish with a crushed cocktail onion.

Wine and Champagne Cocktails

Whether you are looking for a light and refreshing wine cup or the ultimate champagne indulgence, there's plenty of choice in this selection.

Alfonso

4 measures of champagne or sparkling wine
1 measure of Dubonnet
2 dashes of angostura bitters
1 lump of sugar
1 whole ice cube
a cocktail cherry

Put the lump of sugar in a wine glass with the bitters. Add an ice cube and the Dubonnet and stir gently. Top up with champagne or sparkling wine and garnish with a cocktail cherry.

American Glory

3 measures of champagne or sparkling wine
2 measures of orange juice
2 measures of lemonade
whole ice cubes

Place the ice cubes in a chilled tall glass, then pour in the measured ingredients.

Andalusía

3 measures of champagne or sparkling wine
1 measure of sweet sherry
a cocktail cherry

Pour the measured ingredients into a chilled champagne flute and garnish with a cocktail cherry.

Black Tie

1½ measures of champagne or sparkling wine
3 measures of dry white wine
a black grape

Pour the ingredients into a chilled wine glass and garnish with a black grape.

Black Velvet

3 measures of champagne or sparkling wine
3 measures of Guinness

Pour the champagne or sparkling wine into a chilled small beer glass and top up with Guinness.

Buck's Fizz

See photograph on page 102.

2 measures of orange juice
4 measures of champagne or sparkling wine
a slice of orange (optional)

Pour the orange juice into a chilled goblet or large wine glass, then top up with champagne or sparkling wine and garnish with a slice of orange, if liked.

California

1 measure of tequila
2 measures of orange juice
2 measures of pineapple juice
4 measures of champagne or sparkling wine
whole ice cubes

Half-fill a cocktail shaker with whole ice cubes, add the tequila and fruit juices and shake. Strain into a chilled goblet or large wine glass half-filled with ice cubes, then top up with champagne or sparkling wine. Serve with straws.

Champagne Cobbler

6 measures of champagne or sparkling wine
2 dashes of old brandy
2 dashes of lemon juice
4 dashes of sugar syrup
broken ice
slices of fresh fruit

Half-fill a mixing glass with broken ice, add all the ingredients except the fruit and stir gently. Strain into a chilled whisky tumbler half-filled with broken ice, garnish with fruit and serve with straws.

Champagne Cockney

1 measure of gin
½ measure of lemon juice
½ measure of sugar syrup
3 measures of champagne or sparkling wine

Mix the gin, lemon juice and sugar syrup in a chilled champagne flute, then top up with champagne.

Champagne Cocktail

*One bottle of champagne or sparkling wine will make
six cocktails.*

1 lump of sugar
2 dashes of angostura bitters
2 twists of lemon rind
champagne or sparkling wine
whole ice cubes

Place a lump of sugar in a chilled wine glass, add the angostura bitters and an ice cube and squeeze in the juice from one piece of lemon rind. Fill with champagne or sparkling wine, stir gently, then add the second twist of lemon.

Champagne Cup

Serves 4–6

1 measure of curaçao
1 measure of maraschino
2 measures of brandy
1 bottle of champagne or sparkling wine
1 bottle of soda water
slices of lemon and orange and a sprig of fresh mint

Mix together all the ingredients in a chilled jug, adding soda water to taste, and decorate with the slices of fruit and a sprig of mint.

Champagne Punch

juice of ½ lemon
4 teaspoons of sugar syrup
½ measure of Cointreau
champagne or sparkling wine
whole ice cubes

Half-fill a cocktail shaker with ice cubes, add the lemon juice, sugar syrup and Cointreau, and shake. Strain into a chilled wine glass and top up with champagne or sparkling wine.

Cider Cocktail

4 measures of cider
½ teaspoon of sugar syrup
a dash of angostura bitters
broken ice
a slice of lemon

Half-fill a mixing glass with broken ice, add the measured ingredients and bitters and stir gently. Strain into a chilled wine glass and garnish with a slice of lemon.

Claret Cup

1 bottle of claret
¾ litre soda water
3 measures of brandy
1½ measures of Cointreau
1 teaspoon of lemon juice
whole ice cubes
slices of lemon and orange and a sprig of fresh mint

Place the ice cubes in a large jug or glass bowl, add the measured ingredients and stir well. Garnish with the slices of fruit and a sprig of mint.

Fruit Wine Cocktail

See photograph on page 66.

1 measure of dry white wine
1 measure of dry sherry
1 teaspoon of sugar syrup
a few slices of banana
a slice of orange
a slice of grapefruit
a little lemon juice
a little caster (superfine) sugar

Moisten the rim of a saucer-shaped glass with the lemon juice, then dip the rim in caster sugar to coat. Add the fruits, then pour over the wine, sherry and sugar syrup.

Heart Stirrer

See photograph on page 102.
This will serve about 6 people.

6 measures of amaretto
a bottle of champagne or sparkling wine

Place a measure of amaretto into each chilled champagne flute or tall wine glass, top up with champagne or sparkling wine and stir gently.

Red Wine Punch

Serves 4–6

juice of ½ lemon
½ measure of sugar syrup
½ measure of Cointreau
red wine
whole ice cubes

Half-fill a cocktail shaker with ice cubes, add the measured ingredients and shake. Strain into a chilled wine glass and top up with red wine.

White Sangria

5 measures of dry white wine
½ measure of lemon juice
½ measure of orange juice
½ measure of lime juice
½ measure of sugar syrup
broken ice
soda water
a slice of orange
a cocktail cherry

Half-fill a chilled tall glass with broken ice, then pour over the measured ingredients. Add soda water to taste and garnish with a slice of orange and a cocktail cherry.

White Wine Cup

See photograph on page 104.

This should serve about 6 people.

a bottle of dry white wine
1 measure of brandy
1 measure of yellow chartreuse
½ measure of maraschino
whole ice cubes
soda water
slices of orange

Combine the wine, brandy, chartreuse and maraschino in a large jug and chill thoroughly. Top up with soda water, add some ice cubes and garnish with orange slices.

Zingy Fruit Refresher

See photograph on page 103.

4 measures of grapefruit juice
4 measures of orange juice
lemonade
whole ice cubes

Pour the grapefruit and orange juices into a chilled tall glass and add some ice cubes. Top up with lemonade to taste.

Index

essentials

quality and value in a handy pocket-size format

available from all good bookshops